QUESTAR PUBLISHERS, INC.

presents:

the
BIBLE ANIMAL BAND

Singing & Telling the Story of Time & Forever

written by *MACK THOMAS*

illustrations by *'MAGINATION*

and introducing the musicians
FARGO FOX
RAVEY the RAVEN
BLUE STREAK the SKUNK
PILLA PORCUPINE
& HOGTIE the RAZORBACK HOG

THE BIBLE ANIMAL BAND

© 1990 by
QUESTAR PUBLISHERS, INC.
Sisters, Oregon

Printed in the United States of America

International Standard Book Number: 0-945564-36-8

Cover design by DAN RICH

to a man whose heart hears well the Band,

a man of the stars and a man of the land,

a man for many, giving his time,

a man of the mountain, winning his climb

When a sudden breeze
blows down from the mountaintops
and dances in the tree branches
and skips across the lake waters—
you never know what music it might bring
from far away…

Like a trumpet blast from a fox — who wears a green hat and says,

"HELLO! I'm **Fargo Fox**, and we're the **Bible Animal Band**.
We sing and play and tell stories. But not just *any* stories — *Bible* stories!
Bible stories that have *animals* in them!
That's the kind of stories we like best,
since we're animals too.

"Let me introduce the rest of the Band:

"Above me on the perch is **Ravey the Raven** — the brightest, breeziest bird I know.

"Back there on the piano is **Blue Streak.** As you can see,
he's a very special skunk: His stripes are blue instead of white!
Plus, Blue Streak knows more big words than the rest of us put together.
You'll be hearing *lots* of them real soon.

"Below Blue is our sweetheart **Pilla Porcupine** —
wearing, as usual, a lovely pink ribbon.

"Last but not least is the fellow in the middle: **Hogtie the Razorback Hog.**
He's…he's…well, he's just Hogtie — and he knows the Good Book
from beginning to end.

"And now — here's a song *just for you:*"

Oh, we're the Bible Animal Band!
Our sound is sweeping the land!
And we sing it and we play it
right now—we won't delay it!
We sing at your command…

'Cause we're the Bible Animal Band
and we've got YOU in our plans!
Come and meet us, come and greet us!
Come along and you'll complete us!
Come join our happy Band!

THEN FARGO asked the Band,
"What story shall we sing and tell today?"

"How about the long one!" said Blue Streak.

"You mean — The Long One?" said Ravey.
"The one that never ends?
The one that could go on forever?"

(And that's just the song they sang — several times!)

Never gets old, never gets cold,
more exciting the more it's told,
ever growing, ever longer,
always better, always stronger;
sweet as a kiss,
light as a feather,
a story like this
could go on forever
and ever and ever and ever and ever
and ever and ever and ever and on
and ever and on forever!
Growing and going forever!...

"Wait! WAIT!" Blue Streak said, interrupting the song. "We're already going on forever
without truly getting started. Let's go back and begin *properly.*"

"You're right," said Fargo. "So how far back should we go?"

"All the way," Blue Streak answered. "All the way back...
to the very beginning of everything!"

But first Pilla Porcupine had a question: "Why does everything have a beginning?"

"It's because of God," said Blue Streak. "God is the beginning of everything we see:
this grass, that sky, you and me — everything!"

And Hogtie quoted from the Bible: "The Good Book says,
'In the beginning God created the heavens and the earth.'"

"Hogtie, tell us more about that," said Ravey. "How did everything start?"

"All-righty, I'll tell you," said Hogtie. "This story has come down
from our fathers and our mothers, our grandfathers and grandmothers,
and our great-grandfathers and great-grandmothers — the animals of long ago.

"And this is how it goes..."

"NOW IT'S TRUE what Blue Streak says: Everything got started once, and God Himself was the Starter.

"But before that there was nothin' — absolutely nothin'. Why, there was more *nothin'* than you see when you turn out the lights. There was more *nothin'* than you have when you finish your cornflakes and slurp up all the milk. There was more *nothin'* than you hear when you cover your ears and hide your head under a pillow.
So God speaks a few fine words kinda like this: He says,
'Let's *HAVE* somethin' here. Let's have…some *light!'*

"AND WHAT DO YOU KNOW?
Things brightened up that very moment.

"Now that was the first day of the week.
And on Day Two, God says, 'Let's have a *sky!*'
Now there hadn't been a sky before.
But when He said it, then as quick as blinkin' your eye…

"…THERE _WAS_ A SKY, right up yonder!

"Then came Day Three.
And God says, 'Let's have some dry land over *here*,
and we'll keep the waters over *there*'…

"AND RIGHT THERE IT WAS: dry land, up high where the waters couldn't reach it.

"Yep, this world was takin' shape! And how do you think it looked to God?"

"I'll bet it was *beautiful!*" said Pilla.

Hogtie smiled (showing his terrific tusks). "You said it, Sister Pilla!

"And before that day was gone,
God says, 'Let's have somethin' more.
Let's have bushes and shrubs and mushrooms
and vines and shade trees and fruit trees and evergreens
and grass and ferns and flowers — let's have it all!'...

"AND SURE ENOUGH, there it was,
that very afternoon: *green, green* everywhere.

"How do you think all that green looked to God?"

Ravey answered, "I'm sure He thought it was absolutely *stunning!*"

"That's just the word, Sister Ravey."

Then Hogtie continued: "On Day Four, God says,
'Let's have a sun for the daytime, and a moon for the nighttime.
And while we're at it, let's have some twinkly-bright stars too'...

"SO SUN, MOON, AND STARS were there in half a shake.

"Now tell me," said Hogtie: "In God's eyes, how did they shine?"

"DeeeeLIGHTfully!" answered Fargo.

Hogtie laughed. "Indeed, Brother Fargo — DeLIGHTfully bright!"

And he continued: "The next mornin' God looked down
at the lonely lakes and rivers and creeks and the wide open ocean,
and He says, 'There just oughtta be *fish* down there!
Let's have some *fish!*' And before you could say 'pickled oysters'…

"ALLLLL through the waters — FISH! —
a-shimmerin' and a-skimmerin' and a-swimmin' everywhere.
He just uttered the word, and there they were.

"Now," asked Hogtie, "did God like their funny-fishy looks?"

"I would guess," said Blue Streak,
"that He was thrilled to see their gills,
and had a grin to see their fins,
and was regaled to see their scales!"

"You guessed exactly right!" said Hogtie.

And he continued: "Later that day,
God looked out on those lonely, empty skies, and He says,
'There just oughtta be some *birds* up there! Let's have some *birds!*'
And before you could say 'scrambled eggs'...

"ALLLLLL over that sky — BIRDS! —
a-twitterin' and a-skitterin' and a-flitterin' and flyin' everywhere.
God just uttered the word, and there they were.

"Now," asked Hogtie, "was God happy about that?"

"Happy as a lark!" said Pilla Porcupine.

"Yeah, Sister Pilla! — as tickled as fresh feathers!"

And Hogtie continued:
"The next morning God looked out
on the hills and hollers and the fields and the forest,
and He says, 'There just oughtta be...there just oughtta be...
there just oughtta be ALLLLLL kinds of animals out there! Let's have 'em!'...

"AND JUST LIKE THAT, animals were everywhere —
a-walkin' and a-runnin' and a-rumblin' and a-tumblin'
and a-creepin' and a-crawlin'. He just uttered the word, and there they were.

"And God was as pleased as plums with how they looked.

"So there you have 'em: every kind of creature you could imagine,
and all of 'em still wet behind the ears. And before their eyes was a sight unsurpassed:
an unused, unspoiled, just-out, just-right, upstart, up-to-date world —
where *everything* was brand-spankin' new!"

"Just think," said Ravey.
"Every way they turned,
no matter what they saw —
it was all for the *very…first…time!*"

"AH, it was an extraordinary time!"
said Blue Streak. "A beautiful time!"

Fargo agreed: *"Everything* was
first-time, first-hand,
first-class, first-base,
first-choice, first-rate,
first-edition, first-place!"

"Those brand-new animals found
the first four-leaf clover," said Pilla.
"And even the first three-leaf clover!"

"They played the best game ever
of hide-and-seek," Hogtie added,
"for every hiding place was new!"

And up went a cheer
when Ravey declared,
"Everything they tried —
a jump, or a race, or a dive —
was a NEW WORLD'S RECORD!"

"And all around them," said Blue Streak,
"on every fruit tree and vegetable plant —
there was ripe, juicy, delicious food
that no one had ever tasted."

"Those guys," said Fargo,
"were out in front,
taking the lead,
showing the way,
planting the seed!

"They were *first!*"

They felt the first warm sunshine,
they had the first nice day;
they saw the first spring flowers
and cut the first bouquet.

They dug the first potato,
they picked the first fresh fruit;
they squished the first tomato —
to make tomato soup!...

They were first!

First to see the morning breeze
toss and turn the maple leaves

first to blow a dandelion
first to see those seeds a-flyin'

first to climb a willow tree
first to sing a melody

first to see each other's eyes
first to follow butterflies...

They were FIRST!

first to crack a peanut shell
first to learn how onions smell

first to pull a carrot up
first to touch a buttercup

first to view the noonday sun
first to see the rivers run

first to try a swimming hole
first to feel the water cold...*(brrrrr!)*

They were FIRST!

First to watch a pinecone drop
first to climb a mountaintop

first to see a waterfall
splashing down a canyon wall

first to look inside a cave
first to hear an ocean wave

first to see their shadows grow
first to see the sun sink low...

first to see the moon so far
first to see a falling star...

first to feel the night so deep
first to close their eyes and sleep...

THEY WERE FIRST!

"AND WITH EVERYTHING
so strangely new," said Ravey,
"do you think they ever felt afraid?
Why, absolutely not! Because back then,
there was nothing bad in the whole wide world."

"YEAH!" said Hogtie. "For the Good Book says:
'God saw *all* that he had made — and it was *very good.*'"

"Oh!" said Pilla suddenly. "My heart is telling me something!
God made everything so good — because *He's* so very, very good!"

"I believe you're right," said Ravey.
"One has to be good to make something good. I see it this way:

"Because God is good, He makes what is good;
and because God is love, He loves what He makes!"

"DON'T YOU JUST <u>LOVE</u> THAT?" said Ravey. "And since God made *us,*
that means *we're* good! *Very* good! God says so Himself!
How exciting! Why, I feel like *flying!* DON'T YOU?"

Hogtie frowned. "Hold on there, Sister Ravey! Maybe we *do* feel like flying —
but you're a bird and you can do it. We can't!"

"I'd *love* to fly," said Pilla. "But I can hardly jump! It makes me so sad!"

"Same here," said Blue Streak. "I've always longed
to see what's up in the big, blue sky...
But it's only a dream when you can't fly!"

"You know," Fargo said, "it really doesn't seem quite fair—
only *ONE* of us here can fly in the air..."

"Unfair!" said all the others. "Unfair! Unfair!"

"BUT LISTEN, everyone!" said Ravey. "It's true I'm a bird and I can fly;
God made me a flying raven — I'm *happy* I'm a flying raven.
But flying isn't everything!"

"Beats running from dogs," said Fargo.

"But just listen," Ravey pleaded.
"Think about everything *you* can do!
Think of the special ways God made each one of you.
Why — I can't run a race and feel the ground
rushing beneath my feet, like you, Fargo Fox.

"And Blue Streak, I can't 'perfume' the air around me
like you and all the other skunks do.

"And I don't have thorns to decorate with pretty ribbons,
like you, Pilla Porcupine.

"And as for you, Hogtie the Wild Razorback —
I'll never have your strong muscles and your strong good looks!"

"THE FACT IS," Ravey said, "we can be *glad* God made us all different —
different as can be!" (And Ravey sang this song:)

He made a world of difference
where nothing's quite the same,
a big wide world of difference,
a difference I proclaim!

Oh, you don't get honey from horseflies,
and you won't get a shark to sing in the park,
and a bug is never quite your size,
and a sheep will never bark.

Oh, you don't get eagles from snake eggs,
and you won't get a whale to swing in the trees,
and giraffes don't journey on frog legs,
and a snail just will not sneeze.

He made a world of difference
where nothing's quite the same,
a big wide world of difference;
yes, that's the way it came
FROM GOD...
the wonderful way it came!
WE'RE GLAD for the wonderful way it came!

PRAISE GOD for the wonderful way it came!

"FURTHERMORE," said Ravey, "God did a wise thing
when He made all those different kinds of animals.
He made them so they could have lots of animal babies,
and when those babies grew up, then *they* could have babies.
And when *those* babies grew up — *they* would have babies too!
Over and over it would happen, exactly as God wanted.
Because *God loves <u>life</u>!*"

Pilla had another question: "What is *life* anyway?"

"Ahh, *LIFE!*" said Blue Streak.
"Life is *existence,* and *essence,* and *being,* and *presence.*"

"Brother Blue!" Hogtie groaned. "I can't understand you
when you use such big words."

"Then *I'll* explain," said Ravey. "Life is anything that's ALIVE.
And that's the way God likes things: not dead, but ALIVE!
He wants life everywhere. Hogtie, do you remember
what the Bible tells us about that?"

"I surely do," said Hogtie.
"The Good Book says *this* about God and the animals:
'God blessed them and said, "Be fruitful and increase in number…"'
In other words — God was telling those creatures,
'Let there be *a whole lot more* of you —
a MULTITUDE more!'"

"NOW WHEN GOD said that to those very first animals, maybe He was thinking something like this—" (and he led the Band in this song:)

I like you so much—
so VERY, VERY much—
so let there be MORE and MORE of you!

OH!
You're ALL SO FINE—
so VERY, VERY fine—
so let there be a MULTITUDE MORE of you!

It's merrier with more—
it's what you're all here for—
so let there be a whole lot more of you!
YES!
Let there be *a multitude more!*

And all the Band began to sing faster and faster:

More birds
more bees
more monkeys in the trees

more rabbits
more rats
more frogs and dogs and cats

more pigeons
more pigs
more camels eating figs

more fleas
more flies
more eagles in the skies

more cocks
more hens
more lions in their dens

more owls
more coons
more pelicans and loons

more penguins
more seals
more sailfish
more eels

Let there be a whole lot more (YES, more!)
Let there be a multitude more!

More beavers
more bears
more tortoises and hares

more goldfish
more goats
more cougars and coyotes

more mice
more moose
more leopards on the loose

more zebras
more yaks
more egrets on their backs

Let there be a whole lot more (LOTS more!)
Let there be a multitude more!

more weasels
  more otters
    more walrus in the waters

      more crabs
        more crickets
          more thrushes in the thickets

        more peacocks
          more possum
            more elephants so awesome

          more finches
            more pheasant
              more butterflies so pleasant

            more parrots
              more pandas
                more baboons with bananas

              more chicks
                more cheetahs
                  and even more mosquitoes

                    Let there be
                      a whole lot more (MUCH more!)
                        Let there be a multitude more!

"WHEW!" Fargo gasped. "Let's catch our breath.
And while we do, <u>think with me</u> about this Bible verse:

How many
are your works, O Lord!
In wisdom you made them all;
the earth is FULL of your creatures.*

"Just think of the wise and perfect picture God had in mind
when He first made all those creatures and told them to fill the earth—"

(And Fargo sang this ballad:)

Open up your eyes
(the eyes you use for dreaming)
and see with me...

Open up your heart
(the heart you use for feeling)
and sing with me...

See the skies and the seas and the fields
all *filled*
with living things so fair;

for God made life, and God loves life.
Let life be everywhere!

"See it!" said Fargo. "Coming over the hill: a parade of horses, wild and free.
They'll toss their heads as they pass, then gallop down the valley and disappear.
But more will come, on and on, so many you can't count them,
or ever see the last one...."

"And look!" Blue Streak added. "In the stream rushing by us:
fish who jump and splash as they pass, then flow on and disappear.
But more will come, on and on, so many you can't count them,
or ever see the last one...."

"Ahh!" exclaimed Ravey. "Heads up! See the graceful geese flying far above.
They dip their wings and call out as they pass, then fade away in the northern sky.
But more will come, on and on, so many you can't count them,
or ever see the last one...."

Then Fargo and Blue Streak and Ravey sang the ballad together
while the clouds and the river and the grass sang along:

* Psalm 104:24

And the skies and the seas and the fields
are *filled*
with living things so fair;
for God made life, and God loves life…
Let life be everywhere!

"More horses," reflected Fargo…"And more fish," said Blue Streak
with a sigh… "And more geese," added Ravey dreamily.

Then she stood and shouted: *"And more ravens!"*

"And more razorback hogs!" yelled Hogtie.

"And more porcupines!" Pilla said.

"More foxes!" said Fargo.

"And of course," said Blue Streak, as he played a tune on his piano:

I say it now with plunks —
let there be *more skunks!*

They all got going again, faster than ever:

More worms, more whales, more tigers and their tails
more mules, more moles, more gophers in their holes
more gnats, more gnus, more jumping kangaroos!
Let there be a whole lot more (yes, more!)
Let there be a multitude more!

More bison, more blue jays, more burros, more bugs,
more spiders, more sparrows, more swordfish, more slugs
more hippos, more hamsters, more dolphins, more deer,
more robins, more rhinos — *now let them appear!*

(Take a deep breath!)

MOOOOOOOORRRRRRRRE . . .
llamas, lizards, ladybugs, lynx
dingos, donkeys, muskrats, minks
turkeys, trout, shrimp, swans,
beetles, buzzards — on and on!

Polar bears, centipedes, guinea pigs, chickadees,
angelfish, hummingbirds, octopus, chimpanzees,
dragonflies, crocodiles, wolverines, buffaloes,
nightingales, manatees — more of these, more of those!

Let there be a whole lot more (LOTS MORE!)
Let there be a multitude more!

More!

MORE!

MORE!

"AND THERE *WERE* MORE," said Hogtie. "But, you know, something important
was missing: None of those brand-new animals had names!"

"What a shame — to not have a name!" said Pilla.

"What those animals needed," Hogtie went on, "was a Namer.
If you're gonna get a name, you gotta have a Namer. And God knew that.
So not long after He made all the animals, He made something else —
something very special — for <u>this</u> something was a *someONE*.

"And while He made it,
the animals gathered 'round.
They watched God reachin' down.
Wow! What's He doin'? they all wondered,
'cause He was touchin' nothin' more than a dustpile.
But they hushed, and kept on lookin' and lookin'
and lookin' at that pile of dust —
and they saw it change —
into a PERSON!"

"WHO WAS IT, Hogtie?" Pilla asked.

"It was the first man," Hogtie answered. "And he was a sight so bright that all the creatures scurried behind the bushes and trees.

"Of course they still peeked out through the branches."

"And they saw God breathe His breath into that man."

"THEY WATCHED as God showed him the Garden where the man was to live —
a big, luscious, green Garden, watered by a stream as big as four rivers.

"God showed him all the food in the Garden —
far more than you or I could eat if we had twenty picnics every day.

"The man was glad to be in the Garden.
And God was glad to have him there,
and told him to take good care of it.

"And God named the man *Adam.*

"The animals watched Adam walkin' with God and talkin' with God —
just like best friends do, or like a boy does with the father he loves.

"And all the animals had this to say about Adam:
'He's <u>so</u> much like God!'"

"GOD GAVE ADAM lots of good things to do in the Garden.
Adam's first big job from God
was to *give the animals names.*

"God called out to all those creatures, and asked them to line up
and pass by in front of Adam one by one so he could name them something.

"The animals liked every single name that Adam gave.
'That man is *talented!*' they all said.

"And when Adam was through, the animals were so pleased and grateful
that they gave Adam a name in return.

"<u>This</u> was his name from the animals:

HIGH PRINCE ADAM...
EXALTED NAMEGIVER...
CARETAKER OF THE WORLD...
KEEPER OF THE FIELDS...
SUSTAINER OF THE STREAMS...
WATCHMAN OF THE SKIES...
and by the grace of Almighty God,
EARTHLY RULER OF ALL CREATURES."

"THAT'S THE STORY, brothers and sisters,
of how we got our names."

"But that's not all,"
said Fargo. "As we animals know,
the men and women and boys and girls who came after Adam
can always give *more* names to the animals. Anytime and anywhere,
they can give us as many new names as they want.
The more names they give us —
the more we like it!

"In fact, let me tell you all the names I have,
and how I got them.

"One day long ago, while I was racing through tall grass in a meadow,
I was spotted by a boy with a handsome cap. Nowadays, lots of boys and girls
don't know about the special privilege of naming animals, but this boy did.
He called out, 'Wait, Mr. Fox! Wait! I want to give you a name!'
So I stopped at once, right there in the tall grass.
The boy came close to me and whispered,
'Mr. Wild Fox, from now on
your name is:

"'Fargo Ferdinand Fast-foot Funny-face
Fire-fur Fisherfield Fox!'"

THEN BLUE STREAK told his story:

"*My* name," he said,
"was given to me by two girls playing in their treehouse in the woods.
They were very quiet, and I didn't see or hear them as I passed under their tree.
But suddenly they called down to me: 'O skunk — you there — yes, *you!*
We've been watching you, Mr. Skunk, and we want to name you.'
They hurried down from the treehouse and stood beside me.
Looking first at one another, and then again at me,
they said: 'O skunk with stripes of blue,
we give <u>this name</u> to you:

"'Blue Streak True-speak Fuzzy-cheek Every-week
Tell-it-up Smell-it-up Lotsa-spunk Kennebunk Skunk!'"

NEXT it was Ravey's turn:

"I got my name from two boys who were trying to put salt on my pretty tail. However, I was too fast for them. 'We can't catch you,' they said, 'but we <u>can</u> name you. *So your name is:*

"'Ravey Racer Chimney-chaser Looper-fly Lucy-by Salt-free Lauralee Long-feather Ready-ever Raven!'"

"IT HAPPENED TO ME," said Hogtie, "like this:

"One day on Kneecap Mountain, a white-haired granny got after me.
I thought she wanted to catch me and turn me into sausage, so I ran like lightnin'.
I got as far as Slurry Creek, which was flooded,
so I couldn't get across.
I was trapped.

"Granny grabbed me in her arms, took me out in the creek,
dunked me three times, and said, 'Listen here,
you ol' warthog; *I christen you:*

"'**Hogtie Bogpie Pig-sty Knee-high Haggai Malachi
Meshach Shadrach Crackerjack Razorback Hog!'**"

NOW it was Pilla Porcupine's turn:

"I lost one of my ribbons one day," she said, "and I was looking everywhere,
when I heard a man's voice behind me saying,
'Excuse me, ma'am — did you lose this?'

"I turned and saw a hiker holding my ribbon. He'd found it on the trail.
As he tied it back on for me (very carefully, I might add), he said,
'I think you need more from me than this ribbon;
you need a name. *I'll call you:*

"'**Pilla Quilla Marsha-milla Briar-betty Don't-forgetty
Multi-spine Ribbon-shine Friend-of-mine Clementine Porcupine!**'"

"It's great to have fun names," said Fargo.
"And I hope the next boy or girl who sees me will give me even more!"

Then Pilla said, "Oh — my heart is telling me something!"

"What is it, Pilla?" said Fargo.

"It's this," Pilla answered: "God is so good to give people and animals *to each other!*"

"YES!" said Ravey. "God arranged everything so well!
That was clear, right from the start. Adam had a wonderful world.

"And it became a *perfect* world when God made His final creation that week —
He made a woman to be Adam's wife, and she became his closest friend.
Adam saved his best name for her — he named her Eve,
which means *Life.*

"Together, Adam and Eve had everything you could want.
God let His love shine on them, and Adam and Eve could feel that love.
Then, like a mirror, they let their love shine back to God. Adam and Eve were *happy.*

"In the very center of the Garden were two special trees.
One tree always reminded Adam and Eve of God's love for them.
It was called the Tree of *Life,* and it was beautiful. As they enjoyed its fruit,
they would live forever.

"The other tree reminded Adam and Eve how they could give love back to God.
This tree was called the Tree of the Knowledge of Good and Evil.
God told them very clearly *not* to eat the fruit on this tree.
He was saving this tree's fruit for something special,
though Adam and Eve didn't know what.
'Don't eat it,' God told them,
'or else you will die.'

"God didn't want Adam and Eve to die; that would make God so terribly sad!
If they ate the fruit and died, that wouldn't be loving God at all!
But by obeying God, by not eating that fruit,
Adam and Eve showed God
that they loved Him,
and believed Him,
and trusted Him."

"I wish it were true," said Blue Streak,
"that Adam and Eve *always* obeyed God.
But one day, for the first time, they disobeyed.
It was the first disobedience in the world, *and the first sadness."*

"IN THE WARM SKY a hawk circled above the Garden that day.
Suddenly he spotted trouble: The devil — Satan himself,
the enemy of God — was sneaking into the garden.
And he was disguised *as one of God's creatures!*

"Right away," said Blue Streak, "the hawk went to tell the other animals.
'Satan is pretending to be one of us!' the hawk announced.
'How scurrilous!' sputtered the squirrel.
'How disrespectful!' declared the deer.
'How galling!' groaned the sea gull.
'How obnoxious!' observed the ox.
'How brazen!' bellowed the bear.

"*'And just WHAT is that devil-snake doing here in the Garden?'*
they all asked one another.

"Then they saw the reason:
He was headed straight
for Eve, to trick her."

"Right about then," said Hogtie, "the animals had an idea:
Maybe they could warn Eve. They planned how they might do it:
The parrots and monkeys could scream...the dogs and wolves could howl...
the elephants could trumpet...the lions could roar...the donkeys could hee-haw...
the giraffes could wave their long necks wildly from side to side...
the kangaroos and the rabbits could jump backwards...
and the eagles and hawks could fly upside-down.

"But," said Hogtie, "it was <u>too late</u>.
Eve was already listening to that sneaky devil-snake.
The devil-snake, who was a liar, told her awful things about God.
And he told her to go ahead and eat the fruit God told them *not* to eat.

"Eve listened to that devil-snake instead of listening to God."

"SHE ATE the forbidden fruit.

Then Adam ate some too."

"Adam and Eve had disobeyed.
They had sinned. They had turned their backs on God!
Then they ran behind some trees to hide, because they heard God coming."

"IT WAS A FAST FALL,"
said Hogtie, "and the animals saw it all.
The sun was going down now, and it was cooler —
the time of day when creatures come out to run and play and eat and drink.
They saw God walkin' in the Garden. He called out,
'Adam, where are you?'

"The animals turned their heads to the place in the trees
where Adam and Eve had hidden — and they heard Adam tell God,
'I'm hiding because I heard You coming, and I'm afraid, and I'm ashamed.'

"Then a rabbit on the front row remarked,
'That sure doesn't sound like the Adam *I* know.
He sounds lost and scared!'"

Fargo continued the story:
"God asked Adam and Eve if they had eaten fruit from the tree
that He told them not to eat from. They had to admit — it was true.

"The animals watched God having a long and sorrowful talk with Adam and Eve.
He told them that from now on there would be *hurting* and *dying* in the world.
And God used another hard word Adam and Eve had never heard before:
the word *curse.* It was a sad word about the punishment and trouble
Adam and Eve had brought into the world because of their sin.

"THEN GOD made Adam and Eve
leave that beautiful Garden,
and told them they could
never come back."

"THEN," said Blue Streak, "the animals saw a flashing fire—
a flaming sword swung back and forth by an angel!
It frightened the animals,
and they left too.

"The Garden wasn't home for anyone anymore."

Now Ravey carried on the story:

"The animals watched Adam and Eve in their new life outside the garden —
and it was a hard life for them, just as God said it would be.
There was *crying,* and *hurting,* and *dying.*

"Adam and Eve had children.
And soon those children grew up, and *they* had children,
then those children had more children; there were more and more people
all the time.

"The animals thought all these people would start obeying God and loving Him.
But they didn't. After Adam and Eve disobeyed God the first time,
it seemed easier for everyone to keep disobeying God.
The animals saw people stealing, and lying,
and cheating — and even killing."

CURSED... AND CRYING...
HURT... AND DYING...

"THE ANIMALS started hurting too," said Fargo.
"They started dying. And they wondered why.

"Now, a good many of us animals," Fargo pointed out,
"can see better and smell better and hear better than people can.
So when the animals looked out on the world,
they noticed something that people didn't:
the terrible darkness of sin and death.
It covered everything.

"The eagles could *see* the darkness of sin and death —
they said it looked like ugly smoke.

"The horses could *smell* the darkness of sin and death —
they said it stank like something rotten and burning.

"And the deer could *hear* the darkness of sin and death —
they said it sounded like a scream from far down in a deep, dark hole."

Then Blue Streak said sadly,
"Surrounded by that darkness, many animals became
wild and fearsome, and enemies of one another.
They wanted to be friends — but just couldn't.
The lions began killing and eating the deer.
The hawks began attacking the field mice.
The wolves began hunting the sheep."

"There was <u>more</u> <u>and</u> <u>more</u> <u>trouble</u>," said Fargo.

"Things got worse…

"And worse…

"And worse…"

"...AND *WORSE,*" said Blue Streak.
"But soon the animals started watching a man named Noah.
He was <u>so</u> interesting to watch because he was so different from other people.
He continually prayed to God, which nobody seemed to do anymore.
Furthermore, he and his family were building a giant boat.

"One day when the boat was finished, a chipmunk said to a mouse,
"I wonder if that big boat has anything to do with *us?*"
He said that because he saw Noah and his family
loading the boat with the kinds of food
that animals like to eat most —
nuts, and fruit, and grain,
and straw."

"AS YOU KNOW," Hogtie remarked, "we animals can tell when danger is near before people can. One day these animals felt a shaky-shiver go through their bones. They knew an enormous *somethin'* was about to happen —
but didn't know what it was.

"None of the people seemed to notice — none of 'em, that is, except ol' Noah and his family, who were gathered outside their boat."

"All the animals were scared," Ravey said, "yet they couldn't decide what to do. Most of them were still enemies of one another, and they couldn't agree about anything. Even animals of the same kind couldn't agree.

"For example,
lots of the elephants wanted to run to the hills.
Lots of other elephants wanted to run to the valleys and fields.
Lots of others wanted to hide in the forest, or in caves.
Only *two* elephants thought Noah's boat
was the best place to go.

"It was the same with the giraffes,
and the buffaloes, and the monkeys, and all the animals."

Hogtie continued:
"While they were discussin' this,
suddenly they heard a little rumblin' in the ground.
Then they saw a little spark of lightnin' flash across the sky.
It was only a little, but it was the first time these animals
had ever heard earth-rumblin' or seen lightnin'.
That *really* scared 'em!

"So thousands of elephants — and thousands of giraffes and monkeys
and buffaloes and other animals too — ran to the hills.
Thousands ran to the valleys and the fields.
Thousands went hidin' in the forest
or in the caves.

"But a couple of elephants — and a couple of giraffes,
and two monkeys, and two buffaloes,
and two of the others too —
all these ran to Noah
and his boat.

"Noah seemed to be waitin' for all these animals.
He and his family led them into the boat.
When everyone was safe inside,
God Himself reached down
and closed the door."

"THEN THE STORM broke loose," said Fargo, "the <u>worst</u> <u>storm</u> the world would ever know."

Ravey told what happened next:

"The rains kept falling and splashing and pounding on the roof of the boat.
'It sounds like God is crying and crying and just can't stop,'
said a frightened koala bear huddled in a corner
with the other koala bear.

"Noah saw how scared the koalas were,
so he came over to talk with them face to face.
'I know you're frightened,' he said. 'You can't understand
why we're having this terrible storm. But let me try to explain it.
You see, the people God made have all become very bad and disobedient
(which made God sad and sorry). They became so mean
that God had to destroy them.

"'And He had to wash this beautiful world, since it was now so ugly and dirty
because of the people's darkness. God sent a storm and a flood
to wipe away all life — all people and all animals —
on the earth and in the skies.'

"'This was the right thing and fair thing for God to do,' Noah said again,
'for God is always right and fair. But God is also *love,* and He has *mercy* — which
means that in His love He sometimes doesn't give us the punishment we deserve.
God had to send this flood to destroy the earth — but in His love
and mercy, He's *glad* to save some of the people
and some of the animals! He will *not*
destroy everyone!'

"Noah smiled and added: 'That's why *I'm* here —
and that's why *you're* here too.
So let's never forget it!'"

"WHEN THE OTHERS on the boat heard the story Noah told the koalas, then all the animals could enjoy being together again, and being friends. And they sang this song:

"Let's never forget what love can do!
Let's never forget God's mercy too!
We walk, we talk, we sing, we smile,
'cause God has loved us all the while.
His love is so tender;
let's always remember
what God in His love can do!"

"AND AFTER MANY DAYS," said Blue Streak, "the rain stopped!"

"And after many days," said Ravey, "the flood went away!"

"And after many days," said Fargo, "it was time for everyone to leave the boat.

"As they walked away, a deer looked over her shoulder at a lion,
and wondered: *Will we be friends now?*

"A field mouse looked up at a hawk flying above him,
and asked himself: *Will there be peace between us now?*

"A sheep looked at a wolf, and thought:
Can we play together now?

"And all the animals looked back at Noah and his family, and wondered:
Will people always obey God now, and not be bad anymore?"

"THEY ALL WENT AWAY to make their new homes," said Fargo.
"And in the sky they saw the very first rainbow
stretching across the fresh, clean air,
reminding them of a bright
new promise from God."

"The whole world had a second chance," said Hogtie.

"A fresh start!" said Pilla.

"A NEW BEGINNING!" said Fargo.

Ravey carried on the story:

"Now the animals watched as Noah's grandchildren
and his great-grandchildren and his great-great-grandchildren all grew up
and had more children. Once more there were lots of people.
But these people began to call one another bad names,
and to fight each other, and to hurt one another,
and to forget about God entirely.

"One day a raccoon and bluebird were in a tree together, watching the world below.
The coon said sadly, 'People still remember how to disobey God, don't they?'
'Yes,' answered the bluebird. 'I've seen stealing, and lying,
and cheating — and even killing.'"

"The animals were still hurting," said Fargo.
"They were still dying. *And this time they knew why.*

"They looked out on the world
and <u>saw</u> again the thickening darkness of sin and death — like ugly smoke.
They <u>smelled</u> it — like something rotten and burning.
And they <u>heard</u> it — like the sound of a scream
from down in a deep, dark hole."

"WITH ALL THAT DARKNESS," said Blue Streak,
"many animals once more were wild and fearsome
and enemies of one another. The lions were still killing deer.
The hawks were attacking field mice, and the wolves were hunting sheep.

"Things got worse…

and worse…

and *worse."*

And the Band sang this:

Woe…
  woe…
    woe is we!
Our world is a-wasting,
 we're sorry to see;
there's crying and dying,
 it's grim as can be;
we groan in our longing;
 when will we be free?

Groan…
  groan…
    groan…
      groan…
Groan…
  groan…
    groan…
      groan….

"MY HEART is telling me," said Pilla Porcupine,
"that God would have to do a <u>miracle</u> if the people and animals He made
were ever going to have a happy world."

"Yes, Pilla, that's *exactly* what was needed," said Fargo Fox.
"There had to be a miracle of God's love and mercy.
The animals remembered Noah's words,
and they wondered what else
God's love and mercy
could do...."

"What could love do <u>now</u>?...

What would love do <u>now</u>?..."

"THEN ONE NIGHT," said Blue Streak, "electrifying news
spread through all the animal world.
It started in a little town
called Bethlehem.

"All the animals there —
from the sheep on the nearby hillsides
to the cattle and donkeys in the town stables —
were breathless with excitement. A baby had been born,
a child unlike any other the world had ever known."

"The animals watched the baby grow
into a fine, healthy boy,"
said Ravey.

"THEY SAW THE BOY grow into a strong, tall Man.
He was <u>so</u> interesting to watch because He was so different from other people.
He always prayed to God, and told people about God all the time.

"As the animals watched Him they had only one thing to say about Him:
'He's exactly…like…GOD!'

"And there was something even more amazing about Him.
There was no darkness around Him.

"Instead, the eagle could see that this Man was like
a ray of the whitest, brightest light.

"The horses could smell that this Man was like
the clear morning air on a mountaintop.

"And the deer could hear that this Man was like
a happy song sounding in the meadow.

"He was exactly…like…GOD!"

"He was stronger than a lion," declared Fargo.
"Yet as gentle as a lamb!" said Pilla.
"His life," said Ravey, "was pure and shining like a morning star!"

"His name," said Hogtie, "was Jesus — Jesus the Christ, the Son of God.
The animals loved Jesus, and they gave Him other names,
which they found in their memories
from long ago:

*"CARETAKER OF THE WORLD…
KEEPER OF THE FIELDS…
SUSTAINER OF THE STREAMS…
WATCHMAN OF THE SKIES…
and by the right and power of Almighty God,
HIGH KING OF ALL CREATION."*

"They knew," said Fargo, "that if all the people in the world would only *listen* to Jesus
and *obey* Him, surely they could get rid of their smokey darkness!"

"BUT NOT ALL the people listened," said Hogtie.

"One dreary dark night an emergency message
was passed along to animals everywhere:
A songbird in a Jerusalem garden
had watched soldiers come
and take Jesus away!"

"THE NEXT DAY," said Hogtie, "the news was even worse. The birds and mice and dogs and cats and cattle and sheep and camels and chickens in Jerusalem saw the people take Jesus and kill Him by nailing Him to a cross."

"AND BECAUSE a good many of those animals could see better and smell better
and hear better than people could, they noticed what those people didn't.
They saw the darkness of sin and death come rushin' onto Jesus,
coverin' Him with that heavy, ugly, terrible smoke.
It made an awful smell — burning and rotten.
And the sound was like a scream
from the deepest
darkest
hole."

Then Ravey said,
"His white, bright light was put out.
The smell like morning air on a mountaintop was gone.
And the sweet sound of happy music in the meadow was now silent."

"That afternoon," said Fargo,
"a family of skylarks watched from a nearby tree
as the dead body of Jesus was buried in a tomb outside the walls of Jerusalem.
The skylarks were so sad they decided to never sing
their beautiful birdsongs again."

"What could love do <u>now</u>?...
What would love do <u>now</u>?..."

"BUT THREE DAYS LATER," said Ravey,
"on the brightest Sunday morning they'd ever seen —
those birds couldn't help bursting into song! They had seen *the greatest miracle ever:*

"With a flash of bright, white light,
and the fragrance of morning air on a mountaintop,
and the sound of happy music in the meadow — *Jesus had come out of that tomb!*

"He was dead no longer! Jesus was ALIVE!
'In fact,' said the mother skylark,
'He seems more alive
than ever!'

"With the help of the sparrows and the swallows,
the skylarks spread this good news
to animals everywhere."

"FORTY DAYS LATER," continued Ravey,
"on a hill called the Mount of Olives, two rabbits watched
as Jesus talked together with a band of men. These were men whom Jesus called
His *disciples,* men who loved Him and had followed Him everywhere.

"When Jesus finished talking with the disciples, the rabbits saw Him
rise up into the sky, higher and higher and higher,
till He disappeared into a cloud.

"And not long afterward,
animals everywhere could see
that the disciples had changed.
In fact, everyone who loved Jesus
had changed in much the same way.
Now they were like a bright light too —
and like the morning air on a mountaintop,
and like happy music sounding in the meadow.

"They were always telling other men and women
and boys and girls about Jesus."

"AND THE MUSIC in their hearts
came out in strong and happy words—
words that the animals like to remember...."

BEHOLD THE LAMB OF GOD,
WHO TAKES AWAY THE SIN OF THE WORLD!

John 1:29

TO ALL WHO RECEIVED HIM,
TO THOSE WHO BELIEVED IN HIS NAME,
HE GAVE THE RIGHT TO BECOME
CHILDREN OF GOD.

John 1:12

IF ANYONE IS IN CHRIST,
HE IS A NEW CREATION; THE OLD
HAS GONE, THE NEW HAS COME!

2 Corinthians 5:17

CHRIST DIED ONCE...TO TAKE AWAY SINS...
AND HE WILL APPEAR A SECOND TIME...
TO BRING SALVATION TO THOSE
WHO ARE WAITING FOR HIM.

Hebrews 9:28

GOD SO LOVED THE WORLD,
THAT HE GAVE HIS ONE AND ONLY SON,
THAT WHOEVER BELIEVES IN HIM
SHALL NOT PERISH, BUT HAVE ETERNAL LIFE.

John 3:16

(It was time now for this song:)

Look what love's done now!
See what love's done now!

Once upon all time,
once upon all time,
God carried out His special plan;
He sent to earth a special Man —
once upon all time.

Down from heav'n He came,
Jesus Christ by name,
so we could know His special love
and go to live with Him above —
once upon all time.

The Son of God...
the Son of Man...
a special love...
a special plan!

Look what love's done now!
See what love's done now!

(And they sang this one too:)

If God is like this — He's worth believing!
If God is like this — that's very good news!
So have faith in God!
Put everything in it!
And don't waste a minute! There's nothing to lose.

Our God *IS* like this — He's worth believing!
Our God *IS* like this — yes, that's the good news!

So have faith in God! Put everything in it!
And don't waste a minute! There's nothing to lose.

"MY HEART is telling me something!" said Pilla:
"When people follow Jesus, and get rid of that smokey
gray darkness, they can live a life that's bright with <u>colors</u>!"

"Right!" said the others. "Let's sing it!"

(So they did:)

Paint a picture with your life
     and you'll make God glad!
Don't be so glum and so gray
     and so sad!
With a smile on your face
     and the good things you do
make God glad
     and *you'll* be glad too!

Put some <u>color</u> in your life
with the good things you do:

yellow…
     and red…
          and pink…
               and blue…

          and orange…
               and green…
                    and purple too!

Make God glad
     and you'll be glad too!

Happy colors!
     Party colors!
          Crazy colors!
               Rainbow colors!

"OH NO!" said Pilla. "I have a question; a *sad* question!"

"Are you sure we want to hear it?" said Hogtie.

"I'm afraid it concerns us all," answered Pilla.
"We've been so excited because boys and girls and men and women
can be a new creation, free from the darkness of sin and death —
free because of Jesus — but what about the animals?
What's changed for *us?*"

Pilla started crying.

"That's a tough question, and I'm not sure
I know the answer," said Blue Streak.
"Maybe there *isn't* one!" he added.
"That would make me so sad!"

And Blue began crying too.

"Now, now," said Fargo, "don't get so down, guys. There's gotta be a good answer.
We know God is good, and He made us — I'm sure
He hasn't left us out of His plan."

"MAYBE HOGTIE can help us," Fargo said. "What do you think, Hogtie?"

"Well, brothers and sisters," said Hogtie, "as a matter of fact, the Good Book tells us about a beautiful *someday*. And this is what will happen on that someday:

> *'The wolf will live with the lamb,*
> *the leopard will lie down with the goat,*
> *the calf and the lion and the colt together;*
> *and a little child will lead them.*
> *The cow will feed with the bear,*
> *their young will lie down together,*
> *and the lion will eat straw like the ox.'"**

"So none of the animals will be wild anymore!" said Fargo.

"That's right," said Hogtie. "And it's Jesus, the Prince of Peace, who will make it happen.

"The Good Book reminds us," Hogtie continued, "that right now the whole creation is groaning — but that painful groaning won't last forever. The Good Book says, *'Creation itself will be liberated from its bondage to decay, and brought into the glorious freedom of the children of God.'"***

"Hogtie!" said Fargo.
"Now *you're* using such big words!
Let me explain that verse: It seems to say that someday, hurting and death will be taken away from all the animals.
They'll be free! Just like God and God's children!"

"FREE!" shouted Pilla and Blue Streak.
"Won't that be great?"

* Isaiah 11:6-7   ** Romans 8:21

"FREE!" shouted Ravey. "I'll bet you guys could FLY with me!
And I could be a first-class runner! Just imagine it!"

(And they sang...)

So —— fast —— I'll —— be ——
So —— free —— See —— me ——
So —— far —— So —— great —— So —— FREE————

I'll be free as can be — YES! For freedom I'm bound!

"Watch me, boys," said Ravey. "I'm off to the races...

"Running free as can be — I will never slow down!"

"And watch us fly!" said the others...

"Flying free as can be — way up over the ground!"

(And the song kept flowing:)

Singing free as can be — what a wonderful sound!

Living free as can be — loving life all around!

Flying free as can be — way up over the ground!

Running free as can be — we will never slow down!

We'll be free as can be —

YES! For freedom we're bound!

So —— fast —— I'll —— be ——
So —— free —— See —— me ——
So —— far —— So —— great ——

So —— FREE————

SO FREEEEEEEEEEEEEEEEEE!

"But you know," said Fargo, "I want to be <u>more</u> than just fast and free.
I want to be *all* I can be — to be *brave* and *good!*"

"Sing it, Fargo Fox!" they told him.

(And he did, with all his heart:)

Oh, what I would be
if only I could be
all that I should be...
and someday I will!

Strong in God and never afraid,
truly loving all things He's made,
always brave, and always kind,
gentle in heart, and wise in mind,
good to all
and all to the good —
all this I would be if only I could;
all this I would be,
and all this I should.

And this is the thrill:
Someday I will!
Someday soon
I will.

Now this I pray:

In some small way,

let someday start today!

"THERE'S SO VERY MUCH to look forward too," said Pilla.
"But actually, the good things have already started.
Even now God's blessings come to us each day,
flowing down like rivers of sunshine!
We could spend all our days
just praising Him!"

"Amen!"
said Brother Hogtie.
"Just as the Good Book says..."

LET EVERYTHING THAT HAS BREATH
PRAISE THE LORD!...

Psalm 150:6

PRAISE THE LORD FROM THE EARTH,
YOU GREAT SEA CREATURES...
WILD ANIMALS AND ALL CATTLE,
SMALL CREATURES AND FLYING BIRDS...
LET THEM PRAISE THE NAME OF THE LORD,
FOR HIS NAME ALONE IS EXALTED;
HIS SPLENDOR IS ABOVE THE EARTH
AND THE HEAVENS....

Psalm 148:7-13

THE EARTH IS THE LORD'S,
AND EVERYTHING IN IT,
THE WORLD, AND ALL WHO LIVE IN IT.

Psalm 24:1

Then they all sang:

Praise God from Whom all blessings flow!
Praise Him all creatures here below!
Praise Him in heaven everyone!
Praise God! Our life has just begun!

Fargo sighed. "What a song!"

"And what a STORY!" said Ravey.

"It'll go on forever!" said Blue Streak...

Never gets old, never gets cold,
    more exciting the more it's told,
ever growing, ever longer,
    always better, always stronger;
sweet as a kiss,
    light as a feather,
        a story like this
            will go on forever...

and ever and ever and ever and ever
        and ever and ever and ever and on...

                and ever and on forever...

THIS WILL GO ON FOREVER!

ALSO FROM QUESTAR

THE BIBLE ANIMAL STORYBOOK
Written by Mack Thomas / Illustrations by Elizabeth Hagler
(hardbound ★ 224 pages ★ ISBN: 0-945564-35-X)

What did the whale think when God told him to swallow a "yucky" man?
(Find out in "A Whale's Tale")

What did a certain fowl find he had in common with Simon Peter?
(Discover his story in "One Scared Rooster")

How did the lions stay occupied the night Daniel "dropped in"?
(You'll enjoy the evening with them in "The Night the Lions Played")

Where did the ravens find food to feed Elijah?
(Share the suspense in "The Raven Raiders")

What lesson did Noah's dove teach the other animals?
(You'll learn it too in "The Outsider Dove")

YES, THE ANIMALS mentioned in Bible stories have their side to tell — and they do it with fun and feeling in *THE BIBLE ANIMAL STORYBOOK.* As one animal puts it, here are "those great old stories...told in a special way that only the animals know!"

Conveying Bible highlights in the classic, best-loved traditions of children's animal stories, this large-format book is a winner for kids from age 4 to 104.

More than 200 color illustrations bring to life the book's <u>seventeen stories</u>, including selections from both Old and New Testaments.

THE BEGINNER'S BIBLE
TIMELESS CHILDREN'S STORIES
(hardbound ★ 528 pages ★ ISBN: 0-945564-31-7)

THIS #1 CHILDREN'S BESTSELLER has more than 500 color illustrations and 95 stories (from Old and New Testaments), all in a durable book perfectly sized for little hands and laps.

"It's all here and it's all in order—advanced theology in living color and captivating characters. The stories speak for themselves, but kids will want to hear them over and over again. More than just 'stories,' these words and pictures will become part of your child's life."
— **JONI EARECKSON TADA**

"THE BEGINNER'S BIBLE is in a class all its own. I've never seen Bible text and illustrations come together with such magical quality. This is the Bible to help every young child vividly experience God's truth. I wish Norma and I had it when our kids were small. We'll certainly make sure it's available to our future grandkids!"
— **GARY SMALLEY**